AF191866

Inger Kier

Caught in a Childhood

Earlier books:

Kärlek över Atlanten 2016

Match made in Heaven 2016

Dedication to my Dear Mother

© Inger Kier 2017

Förlag: BoD – Books on Demand, Stockholm, Sverige

Förlag: BoD – books on Demand, Norderstedt, Tyskland

ISBN: 978-91-7569-7185

I was 5 years old, when my little brother, 3 years old, suddenly dies. The cutest brother imaginable with lightblonde curls. Why did this happen, my family?

This was a horrible experience. I have been told, that I myself had ear infections and lied to bed. We had many ear infections in my family. It was said, that we "inherited" this after dad, who as a child had many ear infections. I remember, that I often had to go to the cottage hospital in my town with terrible earache for a whole night. The doctor cut a hole in the ear drum and the goods ran out.

This was such a wonderful feeling, when it ran out and the pain stopped.

I cannot only describe it as the calm after the storm or the good for evil or Paradise for Hell.

My little brother and our cousins were out on a pond near our house and suddenly the ice broke and he fell into the water with his legs.

Mom, I don't know if she was there or if the cousins called out for her, got him up out of the water the fastest she could. Later in the evening, he will get high fever, over 105 F degrees.

Mom went with him to the hospital. At that time, no parents remain in hospitals with children, so she left my little brother there. It must have been terrible to leave him, as small as he was.

After a few hours they'll call from the hospital and says he is dead.

He had pneumonia and could not be helped or rescued. At that time there was no penicillin, which could have saved him. I have also heard that he drank water from the flower vase, for he was so thirsty. Is there an after construction or is it the truth? Why was no one there and gave him the water? Is it truth, it is horrible, that it could be like that.

My dad is in Copenhagen and get the message, that his son died and hurries home. One can understand, as trauma this is for my parents.

Dad has told me, that he was flying home from Copenhagen and he was met by a car at the airport, who took him home. After this day are all "dark" in my home. At least I felt so. The furnitures were dark and the walls with them.

We had experienced the II World War, not as in close range but had felt a fear of Nazis to come to Sweden.

Mom pulled down the blind literally! I can think of, this, losing a child, was a disaster for my parents. Something so terrible to you should not occur. But this happened and after this day was nothing alike.

During the war, we had had the dark curtains for windows

black so no light trickling out, as revealed to the enemy, where the cities existed. I remember, Dad came home painted black in his face. He was called up and guarded the islands in the archipelago. He had a semaphore, as he waved to the others called in the islands, if something suspicious was in the air or on the water. He was there in months.

During this time, it was the rationing of coffee, milk, cheese, butter, etc. You have to have ration cards and when you used it, for example, coffee, so you could not buy more that month. Number of ration cards were counted out after, how many children they had in the family. I remember that after the war, I was eating an orange for the first time. It was delicious! Even tomatoes were now eating after the war.

Of course the people knew of the threat from Nazi Germany and a fear, that Sweden would be occupied, as was done with Norway. I remember the camouflaged towers built during the war in our small town, where they, the military, could climb up and see if any enemy was approaching. I remember, that he was in an office, darkened for the enemy and where he also served as a conscripted during war time.

No one was out in the evenings, for it was pitch dark. No street lamps were lit. Black, black ... dark, dark.

I also remember or someone told, that the Nazis had to go by train through Sweden, to get to occupied Norway. How could we allow this in Sweden? We had a right Government, which I believe was very German friendly.

People knew at that time not if, what preceded with the extermination of Jews in Europe and gas chambers, who gassed to death millions of Jews. A Hell on Earth!

No news came from Germany, so people were ignorant of what was happening. Today with fast media "apps", TV, SMS, snapshots, such an event reported in record time to us people.

Hermann Göring, who was Deputy to Adolf Hitler, was

married to a Swedish lady. They often lived in Sweden, when they had a house here.

I read about him, the SAPO shadowed him on Strandvägen in Stockholm. Suddenly, he was missing. He had taken himself off to the Grand Hotel of Saltsjöbaden and later to Sandhamn, where they saw him at a table, looking at charts. They wondered, what he wanted to do.

He meets the love of his life, Carin. She is married and has children, but it places no barriers for their stormy passion. It will be a great scandal in Stockholm high society, when Carin leaves her husband for the German war deputy. (B. Schön, "Hitler's knarkande hantlangare")

He was responsible for the construction of all concentration camps, where Jews were sent, to whom it was said: "work in the workshops there".

Unsuspecting, they had to go off after hard work during the day to the showers in nearby buildings. The showers had no water, gas came out of them. Horrible thought! What a terrible death - choked to death. How had this Evil been able to come to Europe. Complete lack of empathy! Narcissistic leaders like Hitler with such great hatred against Jews, homosexuals, the mentally handicapped, etc.

It was said, that he was beaten as a child by his father. With his bad self confidence, he took the power back and killed millions of Jews with his strong hidden aggressions. How could this happen?

Didn´t they see, what was about to happen? The people of Nazi Germany bewithched and brain washed, that this was the right thing to do, to kill the Jews, for they took jobs from them. Intelligent people, which was in the hand of this mass murderer.

Would this happen today? Yes, we are near there, blaming other people. The fear of terrorist attacks from ISIS and large refugee flows meant, that the weaker suffer even more. A mass exodus from Syria and president Al Assad's killing of its own.

That has done, that we are trying to limit the flow of refugees into our country with conflict within ourselves, "are we doing the right" or do we want to "open our hearts" for those, who need help.

There are two sides of one coin, those who are affected and fleeing mass death in Syria and seeking asylum in our country or people, who have lived for generations in our country, who think, that enough is enough to receive refugees.

European countries closed the borders, it deteriorated for all refugees. Radicalisation has grown and with it - the Hate. It is important to safeguard the security of a country, many decisions generated more hatred.

The reason was, that European leaders created deeper rifts between Muslims and other Europeans.

I cannot forget the images after the end of the II World War, when the Americans arrived and liberated Europe from the Nazis, and showing images of hundreds of dead, naked bodies in pits. The mass execution of innocent Jews! How can there be so much evil in the world? It scares!

I remember, not long ago, that my dad was talking to my American husband, about how happy they were in Europe, when the Americans made the entry into the war and liberated Europe from the Nazis. A joy in all European capitals, where now all ventured out and "confetti" were thrown down from the Kungstornen at Kungsgatan over thousands of people, which celebrated Peace in Stockholm after the II World War.

Peace Day is May 8 or 9 1945, depending on where you live in the world. All hugged each other and the happiness had returned to the people. I have also heard stories about, where unknown people hugged unknown to them and how they would like to see these people many years after, to get in touch with them. After Hell - Paradise will come!

Still, I remember, we played a lot out there during this time. I was very much with the neighbour children, who lived in the townhouse, where I lived. We were down at the barn and watched cows. A bull was tethered behind a yellow House.

I was so scared when I passed this house and made sure that I had no red on me, because as I had heard, he could get angry if he saw red! I passed the bull with fear along the other edge of the road, as far away as possible from the beast - the bull.

Another adventure was to climb down into the cisterns, which were at the barn and down there, we hunted or we trapped frogs. We climbed down a fixed latter straight on the cistern. Down there, there were little fertilizer and frogs. We brought up frogs and played with them.

I wonder, how my mom could let me go away for myself

on these adventures. I was probably around 4 or 5 years old, way too small, to be for myself. She trusted well on the bigger kids to take care of me. I also feel that I had to take too much responsibility for my little brother.

We probably played a lot together but I have memories of, that I am alone with him and responsible for him.

One such occasion is when I'll take him on a sled. He sits in the sledbox, as it was for smaller children. We were going downhills a slope and at the end of the hill, a car is approaching.

The car crashed into our sled I end up under the car and breaking a collar bone. My little brother survived. How could we be alone? Where was my mom?

It felt sometimes insurmountable, to take care of a little brother.

I know that when I was in preschool or Kindergarten, German expression, my little brother went with me. Once again alone with my little brother. I wanted to be for myself and not have a brother to take care of.

Here the annoyance came.

"Why do I have to take care of my little brother?"

On another occasion I had the sled, where my little brother is going with me. We go down a small slope and he falls off and hits his teeth in the hard snow, his two milk teeth are knocked out.

Where is my mom? How could it be like this, that I, as 4-year-old, may take care of a younger brother. I see today immigrant children care for their younger siblings. Why aren't the parents there and take care of their children? Yes, they work. My mom was home and would take care of her children.

My little brother was the sweetest imaginable – with gold curled hair! We had fun together in the nursery we were in.

My parents were probably very happy, to have a son, when my mother lost a son before me, in birth.

Losing a brother, a son, is the biggest trauma one can have in a family. This loss of a small child permeates the entire life in my family. Neighbors afflicted with us and often they take care of me.

As I said before, I experienced everything so dark. My mom, who is inconsolable in her sorrow, is in a dark room and crying. I can not do anything but I guess, that I'm trying in some way to get her attention.

For me, she was not "present". I am trying to get in touch with my mom but she does not see me, hear me. She is in her own cocoon. I don't remember how or what I do. I guess, that I continue my kindergarten, now without my little brother.

I have the memory of his funeral. I got a new, white rabbit fur with matching hat. Mom could not see my little brother dead. Dad goes alone to the hospital and take Goodbye of my little brother.

I have already described, how I was annoyed over my little brother, I got to take care of him so much. Now that he is dead, I got probably much Guilt.

I think that little 5-year-old, thought that my "anger killed him". He was not desirable for me. I felt, how I cooked out of anger, to always have him hanging in to be taken care of.

How cruel can a child be? This will probably be over me, because this guilt I carry with me throughout life.

I have incredibly hard to get angry at anyone. Preferably on my little sister, who comes to life 11 months after my brother's death. My sister insists that I never get mad at her. It is true, I do not want conflicts, would rather go away, hard to be confronted by one angry person.

But I carry a guilt with me, that my annoyance and anger towards my little brother has "killed" my little brother. There is nothing I am talking about but probably my parents notice that on my behavior. I never talked with my parents about what I felt. Life goes on.

One month after my brother's death, mom and I are in the laundry room. I stand by the mangle and let my left hand follow the sheet in the mangle. There is no grating. Weird!

Suddenly my entire arm got into the mangle – up to the armpit! I have memory of that it hurted a lot and scar on my arm is still there – as a memory of this trauma!

My mom has the presence of mind to turn off the electricity. Somehow we came to the hospital. They bandaged my arm and kept it in a plaster cradle. I have terrible pain.

I know that I lay in a bed below my parents double bed at nights. Screaming and crying, then I have terrible pain. I hear my mom still lull:

"vuuush, vuuush, vuuush"

over and over again. I get a scar on the forearm after this accident. My inner bone of the forearm was soft, because I was little, so nothing was broken but the horrible pain I can feel even today. I have asked me, why this is happening, my arm goes into the mangle, literally.

I wanted to be dead instead of my brother. I turn the anger into myself – and hurting me. I have unconsciously so much guilt that I am hurting me. Should I not be alive?

Or is there a way to get my mother's attention? We have

never talked about this in my family. I have never asked. Somehow I have protected my parents. They were so sorry about my brother's death, so I probably walked on tiptoe after this.

No one goes unnoticed by this tragedy. My mother mourns and I feel abandoned by my mother. She can not help it. She needs to get through the grief herself. Any outside help, crisis therapy, did not exist at the time.

So my little sister arrives to the world, the cutest little sister. I loved my little sister so much.

Of course mom was very busy with my sister. We have moved to a new house, to make a break from the old one, and as I think, we cannot remember the terrible, when my brother passed away. I know, I longed to be back to the old site, where I have my best friend Stina.

I'll take the bike, 6 years old, and bike away. All by myself, in the streets, across the railway, and bike on the side of the cars.

When I arrived Stina's mom called my mom and told her that I was there. Why did I bike away? Why is my childhood friend more important than my mother? Is it so, that I feel, that my mom doesn't care about me? She has a little one to take care of now! Maybe I already go my own and separate from my mom?

Here the big horse Brunte is coming downhills to our house with new milk pot, which will be put on the steps of our house. Every morning the driver put the milk pot on the stairs. I may come along and sit on the driver´s seat along with the driver. I help him carry out milk pots.

We drive down to the station, to load packages. I feel sometimes the intense smell, when the horse "farted" or, when urinating, a terrible odor, and I kept my nose.

I have probably felt very abandoned by my mother, and I can think of, that I give back in any way against her. The only power I have as little towards her, with the FOOD!

I reject her food! She makes the most delicious food for me and begging me:

"Eat this good food!".

No, I let her do not persuade me. I say stubborn:

"No!"

The only thing I eat at this time is spaghetti with sausage. Also my sister gets to eat and my buddies! Somehow, I've been taking power back from my mom. I am a little one and do not understand my behavior. Refusing to eat! Anorexia?

I turned my love for mom to be a hatred against her, for she abandoned me, when I was a kid. I must have felt so alone after my brother's death and wanted to have my mothers love and solace. She was not for me, she had enough of her own sadness of a son who passed away. Shortly afterwards, my little sister got born.

I was really skinny during this time. Looked like a plank and "Plank" I was called into my teens. I had no boobs as my friends. I starved myself. Maybe this was a way to examine myself from my guilt. My little brother had died, because I was so mean against him! That is, what a little child think.

"I should not eat, when my little brother died. I was not worth the food!"

But more, it was, I felt, to make my mother sad and not eating her food. I would have been sorry that she was not there for me. Now I wanted to give back. My feeling was, that she abandoned me, now I wanted to disappoint her.

Now I am 7 years old and starting school. Exciting! I love

my teacher! I thought, it is fun to go to school. I studied my psalm verses, to be able to know by heart. To answer our questions, we need to stand up. Discipline in schools at that time.

Every morning we had morning meeting and sang a hymn. Our teacher didn't speak, until it was quiet in the class. She could stare hard at the boys, when they didn´t sit still or talked loudly.

I also remember, that Sara and I went through the back area, home from school, and at the same place every day three boys in our class were hiding, who rushed forward and kissed us!

Did we want this, beacause we went the same way all the time and we let them kiss us.

I remember that feeling was: "filthy"!

They wrote love letters to us. Maybe I wanted to have this attention. I remember mom found a love letter from a guy and phoned his parents and asked them to talk to their son. Words like "fuck", "cunt" was in this letter and those words are very ugly at the time. I have never used those words.

I'm walking home alone from school up to our house. I remember that I was afraid to walk past a yellow house with red gables, as these labour houses were allover, where an old man was sitting on the porch. I thought that he looked so strange to me. I passed fast .

Another time, I had the company of a few older schoolmates. I had my sled and suddenly they gave up on me and pulled me off pants and pandies. Why were no adults close and seeing this? They humiliated me.

I got scared and started to cry. I I told my parents, when I got home. My dad got in touch with one of the girl´s dad and talked about, what they did with me. After this they stopped harassing me.

In elementary school, we had a wonderful teacher, who I loved. She was also friends with my parents. I got very good grades. The ratings were from (A) to (C) at the time, where A was "very good".

Once the teacher stopped all teaching an afternoon, to find out, what happened, why the girls were screaming, and why it's been so terrible life on the break. This happened on the breaks, that the boys took us on the genital area and we rescued us downstairs against the girls ' restroom. We shouted and we do not want to be touched "down there". The boys would not let us be. Their hormones had woken up! Sexually harassing would it be named today.

How has it become today, in our Sweden? Is there no respect

for the woman anymore but she has become a victim by empathy disturbed men, who using women for their own desire. How could it be like this? The female, the woman, has been giving birth to the men, otherwise they wouldn´t be alive, if you speaking hard. A woman should be honoured because they have been giving birth to the men to the World.

In stead many muslim women have to hide in a burka, a coat, which is covering her body. Nothing of her body will be seen, which can awake men´s desire.

Where is the border to not "touch", where it is no agreement? Not to use a woman for their own sake. Where has this borderless attitude come from?

Yes, I can agree, in some way, there is no present dad, in these mens´life. No father to identifie with. But we women cannot accept, that this is happening, more sexually abusing and more rapes. We must react!

I remember that it was a tense atmosphere in the classroom. The teacher wondered, what happened, why we girls were screaming? No one said anything. This was going on probably for an hour. It was very unpleasant atmosphere. In the end I handed up my hand and walked up to the teacher.

"They do like this", I said and show my hand against my sex. The teacher thanked me, because I was brave to tell, what happened. After this the teacher began to teach again.

30 years later, we had a class reunion. We had not seen throughout this long period.

A male classmate tells me that I was the reason that he served time in prison and I ruined his life. I felt shocked and afraid of, what he says. I'm being accused of something that happened in the 6th grade. After the episode of boys' touching us and where I told about, what happened, the teacher takes contact with this boy's parents, and he gets the punishment of any kind. He says that he has been in foster care and has gone in and out of prison. He wants to put the blame on me.

"How could you tell our teacher, what we guys did!"

"It's your fault that I ended up in prison!"

I can't stay here, he offends me. I go home from the party after this. I get accused for something I did long ago, and I feel that this man has a lot of hatred against me. The whole family was "broken" and did not doing well socially. There were problems in the family. Here he wanted to burden me a liability.

I lived in a better area of wealthy families, where fathers were managers in our large

International Ironwork. We went to school with the children of the workers in this Ironwork and they crowded together in one room and kitchen.

Were they jealous towards us, who had the better and lived in these big houses?

Of course!

It was a community with large differences between civil servants and labours. I know, how it looked inside the labours´ houses, when we had a paper collection in elementary school. When we knocked on these houses and went into the kitchen, to retrieve old newspapers. Often they had a wood stove and no refrigerator. Privy was in the yard. They had no bathroom.

Once a month the class went to the bath house, so that children could bathe and be cleaned. Thick bath women washed us. I remember a sign:

"Do not Spit on the Floor".

I thought, "who spits"?

But now I'm in my lifetime seen some men, not all, spit! So disgusting, they spit everywhere! Is there any territorial thinking they have? Or why do men spit? Why do they not use a handkerchief to spit into.

This distinction between civil servants and workers accommodation, I felt, when I grew up.

We are just four in my family and have many rooms, bathrooms, stove and fridge. We are privileged. I just play with the kids from my area. I get a little insight into how working families live, then we the whole class goes to a girl, who has been away from school over a month. She lives in one of the labour house. We believe she has become pregnant in this young age of 12 years. We have seen her be together with guys.

They are the children themselves! I, in my innocence, did not even know, how to make a baby.

I know that mom was reading from a book, when I was about 7 years old, about "how the father put his thing in the mother's female thing". It was not something you talked about in my family but I could of course see written words on park benches as "pussy", "dick" and drawing organs. This was ugly for me.

On another occasion Sara and I found condoms in a park near me. We thought: "Have they done this?", so close to us. "Ugh," was the reaction of us but also we were excited over this.

When the class was on class trip down to Helsingborg in 6th grade, the matured girls were with guys. They were "dating", as we said, they were a couple.

I was astonished, what they did and I think, they "slept" with the guys. This was so far from how I was brought up.

"You'll keep on you!",

"Don't come home with a kid before you married you!"

This meant, that I kept a distance to the guys. I made myself unavailable and "cool".

Only in high school, I had a date with a guy. Innocent kisses - never mind that I "slept" with him.

Now that I look at, how it really was, when my little brother died.

I can also understand, how this affected my mom. She became very overprotective of us. Of course, she was afraid that we also would die. Especially my little sister she overprotected much. Every time she got ear infection, she got to stay in bed for a long time and with cotton over the ear, to provide warmth to the ear as well as the scarf around the neck.

I think, my mom had severe guilt, that her son died. When relatives as grandma, dad and close relatives were hospitalised, she was there every day, to take care of them, She had been leaving my brother in the hospital – and he died. She wanted to be in the hospital and make sure, that the relatives did not die. It was her way to process the blame and grief of her son. I know that my mother had very difficult with the loss of a child. She was always afraid, when I went away, that something would happen to me. She was afraid, that I would die from her. She didn't want us driving cars on the road. Any time she wanted us to be at home, so she knew where we were.

As I had, as a psychotherapist, many clients

with similar symptoms as my mother, I understand, that mom had been helped by therapy. That she had gotten through her trauma in a therapy. Instead, we didn´t talk about my little brother. Poor mom! She had it not easy, perhaps the most with me now, when I was growing up. I think I defied her admonitions and was very bold and adventurous.

I remember, after I got Mononucleosis infectionis, "kiss disease" on a study trip to England, where I kissed a guy, I was with and gotten this terrible infection with sore throat, an event: I was not allowed to meet anyone, for I could infect them. The guy I dated in high school came to our summer house and stood outside the window, for he was not allowed to enter.

When I got better, we could, he and I, walk together to a beach. There we could be kissing on the lonely beach. After an hour on the beach, my dad, sent by my mother, and tells me to instantly go home. I thought it was particularly embarrassing in front of my boyfriend, that they treated me in this way. A control over me!

Another time, when I was studying Psychology at the University of Uppsala, I had my boyfriend sleeping over in my place, when we hear someone call the door.

When you are at a University, literally, so you sleep long and sleep in the mornings. You'll study at night! Or? Suddenly, we hear a key into the lock. We have had time to dress. Mom is there. She had contacted the janitor, who have key and can open my door.

Yet another humiliating actions against me by my mom. She has not contacted me, that she should come to Uppsala. I feel like a little child. Also, I had a boyfriend sleeping over, what would she think, my mom. Yes, I seem to be very controlled by my mom. She doesn't let me go.

I defy her and do as I like, but still I have a conflict within me. This wouldn't mom love, if she knew. But I have my life! Yes!

ANALYSIS

I have in this book revealed what the "rejection" in early childhood can do with a child who unconsciously develop pattern in adulthood.

I have had clients in psychotherapy, who felt rejected in childhood. They have at each rejection from the girl, guy, felt the same anger, protest that in childhood.

Take these men, who received a "No" from a partner or who have been abandoned. This can cause strong anger in him. An anger that sometimes can kill.

Watch these men, who cannot take a "No" to either intercourse or relationship, whatever it may bring with them. A fury to be abandoned, that they kill the partner, when that one wants to separate or divorce.

These men have probably an early separation from mom, who's done much pain. A feeling of not "living", but "dead" without mom or without partner.

Or to have been beaten. The child has no trust in adults and must "read" the environment, whether they are angry or happy. Or early have been rejected or criticised, demonstrates strategies among the client, self-fulfilling prophecy, i.e. to repeat the situation, which was in childhood. To put themselves into the situation of the same feeling as in childhood:

"Nobody likes me",

"They leave me"

"It doesn't get any better"

When a child is experiencing, that they are not worth anything, or may never get praised, more criticism - then it becomes hopeless.

We expect failure, then there will be failure.

If someone praises us, and we do not recognise this, we question the praise and we turn it to be: "you're not worth anything", what is the usual pattern, that they are not worth anything.

It means that we will return to this pattern, that we recognize. To be seen, get confirmed does not belong to this client's reality.

When I was working in Psychiatric Clinic I had a meeting with a 10 years old guy. I had a very good contact with him. Once I got too close to him and he got furious and began throw chairs and table towards me.

This guy had never had closeness in his life or anybody loving him. He has never been hold and he got his feeding bottle in a bed, when he grows up and nobody there for him. When I now show him some friendly contact, he got mad and change the pattern to be, what he knew. Everybody afraid of him and he is not worth to be loved.

In therapies, I have several times, heard from the client:

"I'm not good"

"I can not do"

I may point out several times on his/her opportunities and good sides, until he/she can accept this without defense. It sits so firmly rooted, to not be worth anything!

My reaction against my mom was anger, because she didn´t see me. I felt rejected by her. So somehow I get a strategy, to now reject her when she gives me food. I reject her food, don't eat it. Anyway, I want to give back, so she must feel, what I felt, when she had no time for me, when I was little. But everything I did, was unconsciously.

If I go out with an attitude within myself,

"I can do this, it will be so".

Positive expectations become as I expected. If I instead hear my parents say, "you can't do it", which is of course negative expectations, and I'm not going to do it, as the negative expectations were.

Same thing when I was writing this book, I hear my Swedish teacher say:

"That's no good, you can't write", so the confidence was at zero to write essays in high school. I had to go and practise extra with my Swedish teacher. Negative expectations becomes negative. I didn´t believe in me.

Instead I turn on this now, as I write:

"Of course, I could write a book"

and takes a positive view of myself. Those who criticise me, I think to myself, "Joykiller!" They would not let me have the pleasure, but I will keep the joy and let me not be affected.

Or as my American husband said to me:

"How beautiful you are!"

"Me? No, I'm not beautiful!"

In Sweden, this is normal, not to believe in yourself – the Jante law: "You will not believe, that you are something".

In the United States, it is the opposite, they get really to learn, they are something and that they can. They are trained early on, to reference for the class and the teacher gives praise and show the possibilities instead of giving criticism and view on the problem. I may be hard, but I saw it so clearly, when I worked in school in the United States. So my American husband said:

"Say Thank you, when you receive a compliment."

What I learned in the United States, not to go in defense and say, "I am not beautiful", instead I said "Thank you!"

If I think the idea that "nobody likes me", the people keep a distance to me and feel the negative energy. It's like I'm thinking the self-fulfilling prophecy!

71

If I instead shows, that I enjoy myself, I like myself, I will radiate that and I get attracted to the people. People perhaps stop and talking to me.

If I instead think, I'm not anything or I´m not like myself, people avoid me. I think it and create the situation, so no one likes me.

How can we turn this around? When the entire Life heard that: "you are nothing", You don´t know anything".

Well, you can, if you change the attitude to yourself: "I can".

It may be a Mantra:

"I can"

"I want to"

"I'm good"

or put up a Motto on the wall or the fridge:

"I CAN"

"I'M FINE"

"I CAN HANDLE"

Many times, you know, when you walk the street, that you radiate security and pride in yourself and you can see, the people approaching you instead of turning you a back. They might stop and talk to you.

What a lovely emotion, to suddenly be loved and appreciated for who you are.

You can thus turn the attitude against yourself and you can be attractive by people, for you radiate confidence and self esteem.

In therapies, I have many times had clients who had partners who abandoned them. The anxiety that comes from it – to be left.

The first abandonment might you felt when you were left at Daycare. You cried and cried and longed for mom. You didn't think she would come back, but she did.

I have many times explained for clients, that it is not good to let a child be in Daycare before 1.5 years old. They are in symbios with mom up to that age. If they separate earlier, they get "half" a person with no border between itself and mom. That will result in difficulties to see border to others. Many times kids develop behavior problems and problems with the border to others.

They have difficult to see "both – and" sides in themselves. Instead they see "either – or" sides in themselves. I.e they believe to see negative sides in themselves and positive sides in others. A kid who has separated later from mom, can see both the positive and negative sides in themselves.

That´s why I have difficult to understand, why moms in USA has to go back to work after 6 weeks and leave the baby. That could not be good for the little one.

More strange is that USA doing this knowing that all Psychodynamic therapy is developed in US and telling, that the baby is symbios with the mom up to 1.5 years old.

In Sweden a mom is allowed to be home with the baby up to 1.5 years old. That is good and the kid got to separate from mom at that age. And it has "both – and" sides then, hopefully.

Worse is, of course, if the mother died from one, when you are little.

In such cases, one can surely be afraid to go into a relationship for fear of losing someone.

Many times I have asked in therapy client who sits abandoned,

"Can you see yourself to leave your partner?"

They have not thought about that but sitting paralyzed by grief. When they then tried at first to watch mentally to abandon and what they want to do, they can do it practically later.

Many times they have experienced, that partner is now seeking their company again and want to come back. Often, the client becomes attractive for the partner, that it manages itself and is not the "clinging" partner anymore. Now he/she becomes interesting.

Then the question of whether they want to continue together or the client discovered, that it was not so bad to be alone and feel a pride to be for itself. They have turned the issue into an opportunity instead.

Maybe we should watch more and more problems, that they are not so dangerous, that we don't have to ask someone for help, what to do, but they can become opportunities. Problems can be solved.

During my high school, I had a classmate, who ate lunch with us.

One day, it was too much for me. My friend always had the better score of tests. Mom was impressed with and what I felt then was, what I did in the tests were not of value. I was constantly compared with her.

"Oh, you doing so good!"

She told my classmate.

One day I told my mom, I did not want my classmate

eating lunch in our house anymore but I do not think, I explained why. I would of course say:

"You just praise her and I'm not worth anything".

Here and now I was standing up for me.

What can happen in a family after someone's death? I think you should not hesitate to receive crisis therapy, to put words to your grief and your feelings, if you have been affected. I have tried to explain what happened to me, when I lost my younger brother.

I also feel that I am blaming my mom too much, that´s giving me guilt at the same time, but I have to get an explanation as why I got to become what I am today.

My mom had nice, positive characteristics. I knew that she loved me and wanted me well. She was there for me, when I needed her. She couldn´t help, what happened my little brother.

One such occasion was when my husband left me for another woman.

I remembered, that I called her every day and cried and she was there for me all the time and listened to me.

I miss her so much but life must go on after the parents´death.

My thought is that maybe my story will help others. I dared to talk about me, as a psychologist, perhaps that makes, that others dare to talk about themselves and their problems.

They may realize that they need the help of a psychologist to be led in the therapy to see themselves, to put words on the issue. To see their own defense, formed, for they do not want to see the terrible stuff, as happened in the past.

Sometimes the total denial will be there, what happened in their childhood. But in therapy after a while, you can suddenly see what happened in one's early childhood.

For me it has been uplifting to see, why I was "caught" in my childhood, and see the strategies developed to move on after my brother's death.